Romeo and Juliet

Adapted by Conrad Murray with contributions from Lakeisha Lynch-Stevens, Khai Shaw and Kate Donnachie

methuen | drama

LONDON • NEW YORK • OXFORD • NEW DELHI • SYDNEY

METHUEN DRAMA
Bloomsbury Publishing Plc
50 Bedford Square, London, WC1B 3DP, UK
1385 Broadway, New York, NY 10018, USA
29 Earlsfort Terrace, Dublin 2, Ireland

BLOOMSBURY, METHUEN DRAMA and the Methuen
Drama logo are trademarks of Bloomsbury Publishing Plc

First published in Great Britain 2024

Cover image: Diala Brisly

A catalogue record for this book is available from the British Library.

A catalog record for this book is available from the Library of Congress.

ISBN: PB: 978-1-3505-0755-5
ePDF: 978-1-3505-0756-2
eBook: 978-1-3505-0757-9

Series: Plays for Young People

Typeset by Mark Heslington Ltd, Scarborough, North Yorkshire

To find out more about our authors and books visit
www.bloomsbury.com and sign up for our newsletters.

Romeo and Juliet

A Polka Theatre production made with Beats & Elements
Created and directed by Conrad Murray and Lakeisha
Lynch-Stevens
Co-created by Kate Donnachie and Khai Shaw

Romeo and Juliet was originally commissioned and
produced by Polka Theatre, and had its first performance
on 2 March 2024

Original Cast

Conrad Murray – **Capulet / Multi-rolling**
Lakeisha Lynch-Stevens – **Montague / Multi-rolling**
Kate Donnachie – **Juliet**
Khai Shaw – **Romeo**

Understudies

Paul Cree – Montague
Aminita Francis – Capulet
Nadine Rose Johnson – Juliet

Creative Team

Set and Costume Designer – Erin C. Guan
Sound Designer – Simon Beyer
Lighting Designer – Jonathan Chan
Movement Director – Jonzi D
Dramaturg – Lisa Goldman
Stage Manager – Simon Beyer
Set Construction – Basement 94

For Polka Theatre

Artistic Director	Helen Matravers
Executive Director	Lynette Shanbury
Head of Production	Adam Crosthwaite
Head of Creative Learning	Polly Simmonds
Head of Development	Sarah Ruff
Head of Sales and Marketing	Sara Hijazi Greenwood
Head of Finance and Admin	Bernadette Cava
Head of Operations and Visitor Services	Woonie Chan
Senior Producer	Kate Bradshaw
Technical Manager	Peter Hatherall
Theatre Technician	Fergus O'Loan
Wardrobe Manager	Annie James
Associate Director	Roman Stefanski
Community Engagement Manager	Fran Chabrel
Participation Manager	Heidi Pointet
Schools Relationship Officer	Lizzie Corscaden
Community Officer	Jemima Deboo-Sands
Marketing Manager	Julia Canavan
Marketing Officer	Victoria Dowding
Marketing Assistant	Rebecca Short
Sales and Ticketing Manager	Laura Perry
Sales and Ticketing Supervisor	Alexander Benjamin
Memberships and Events Manager	Katie Neame
Trusts Relationship Manager	Lizzie Lord
Events and Campaigns Officer	Amy Sherlock
Senior Finance Officer	Gloria Mason
Visitor Services Manager	Chris Hoare
Volunteer Coordinator	Ray Standeven
Buildings and Operations Manager	Mark Blythe
Commercial and Hires Officer	Ross Bonny
Café Manager	Bruno Fawzi Izem
Café Supervisor	Jaeeun Jung

With huge thanks to the practitioners, facilitators and volunteers who work so hard at Polka to make sure we empower and inspire children daily.

Conrad Murray – Co-Director, Co-Creator and Performer (Beats & Elements)

Conrad is a founding member and artistic director of Beats & Elements. He is a theatre maker, director, musician, writer and composer. He also founded and has lead the BAC Beatbox Academy since 2008, innovating in hip hop/beatbox theatre with various projects.

He was recently the musical director and composer on Michael Rosen's *An Unexpected Twist*, book by Roy Williams. His production with the BAC Beatbox Academy, *Frankenstein: How to Make a Monster* received 5-star reviews from The Stage, The Guardian and others. It won the Off West End award, Total Theatre award, and was the highest rated show of the Edinburgh Fringe and won pick of the fringe at the Adelaide Fringe Festival. It was also adapted into a BBC film in 2020.

Conrad was musical director on Pilot's *Crongton Knights* which was picked as one of the top theatre shows of the year by The Guardian in 2020.

Conrad was chosen as part of The Stage's top 100 people in their 2020 list which highlighted his show *High Rise eState of Mind* with his theatre company Beats & Elements, and a finalist in The Arts Foundations theatre makers category. He was beatbox coach on Giles Terera's *The Meaning of Zong* for Bristol Old Vic.

As director he worked on Connor Allen's 5-star autobiographical grime theatre experience *Making of a Monster* for the Wales Millennium Centre.

He is currently working with director Marc Jobst (*One Piece*, *Daredevil*, *Witcher*) on a musical film *Home*.

In 2022, his first published works were published by Bloomsbury/Methuen Drama, *Making Hip Hop Theatre* and three original texts *Beatbox & Elements: A Hip Hop Theatre Trilogy*. His most recent production *The Pied Piper – A Family*

Hip Hop Musical won an Off West End award for Best Music and is on tour in 2024/25.

He has collaborated and/or made work for various venues and institutions including Battersea Arts Centre, the National Theatre Studio, the Lyric Hammersmith, Mountview School of Theatre Arts, LAMDA, the Tate, Royal Central School of Speech and Drama, Camden People's Theatre, HOME Manchester, Roundhouse, Theatre Royal Stratford East, UCL and The Courtyard Theatre.

Lakeisha Lynch-Stevens – Co-Director, Co-Creator and Performer (Beats & Elements)

Lakeisha is an actor, writer and director who has performed in and co-created children's shows for many theatres and platforms UK-wide. She is the director of Camden Youth Theatre, performer/co-author of *High Rise eState of Mind* and has co-created/performed in Rhum and Clay's *Everything Has Changed*. Credits include ITV featured children's short *High Above the Sky* (First Light Award/Mew Lab/SPID) and *Birthday Wish* (British Urban Film Festival).

Kate Donnachie – Co-Creator and Performer

Kate is an actor, singer, and beatboxer from South London who graduated from Italia Conti as a Carlton Hobbs Bursary Award runner-up and Alan Bates Award finalist. She has been part of the BAC Beatbox Academy since 2014, training and performing at various venues from the Royal Festival Hall to Latitude Festival. She is now facilitating the next generation of beatboxers working closely with Conrad Murray across the country and in some of the UK's top drama schools. She has toured with their 5-star show *Frankenstein: How to Make a Monster* and is in the development processes of their next hip hop theatre shows.

Theatre credits include *Hansel and Gretel* (The Globe Theatre); *Pied Piper* (BAC Beatbox Academy); *Unexpected*

Twist (Children's Theatre Partnership and Royal & Derngate Northampton co-production national tour); *Crongton Knights* (Pilot Theatre national tour); *Frankenstein: How to Make a Monster* (BAC Beatbox Academy national tour); *3 Years, 1 Week and a Lemon Drizzle* with her actor/writer sister, Alexandra Donnachie (Underbelly, Edinburgh Festival); *Return to Elm House* (Battersea Arts Centre); *Aladdin* (Lyric Hammersmith, Best Supporting Artist in the UK Pantomime Awards).

Radio credits include *China Towns* (BBC Radio 4).

Khai Shaw – Co-Creator and Performer

Khai is a multi-disciplinary, multi-award nominated actor/performer and writer. Having performed since the tender age of four years old, he has worked on some prestigious projects including *Casualty*, *The Lion King* (West End) and with the BBC Concert Orchestra.

A graduate of the prestigious Brit School and Rose Bruford College, he is a three-time Off West End award nominee, one-time Black British Theatre award nominee and a one-time Stage Debut award nominee for roles in productions like Pilot Theatre and Alex Wheatle's *Crongton Knights*, Arinze Kene's *Little Baby Jesus*, Frantic Assembly's *I Think We Are Alone* and most recently, *Alice in Wonderland* at Brixton House. He has also worked with the Royal Shakespeare Company, Amazon Studios and as a voiceover artist, has worked with the likes of the BBC and Audible.

As a writer, he is a Talawa Writers' Group alumni and a Soho Writers' Lab cohort member. His work was seen at Talawa Firsts 23 and will be back at Talawa Firsts in 2024. He is working on his debut short. At seventeen, he co-founded the theatre company Nuu Theatre with Ben Quashie and other members. They have since gone on to collaborate with the English Touring Theatre Company and the Bush Theatre.

Paul Cree – Understudy (Montague/Multi-rolling)

Paul is a performer, rapper, poet and co-founder of hip hop theatre company Beats & Elements. He's performed around the UK at a variety of festivals and events such as Bestival, Latitude and the Edinburgh Fringe. His work has featured on BBC 1Xtra and BBC London. He has written and performed two solo shows: *A Tale from the Bedsit* (2013) and *The C/D Borderline* (2016) as well as co-writing and performing in the critically acclaimed Beats & Elements shows, *No Milk For The Foxes* (2015) and *High Rise eState of Mind* (2019.) In 2018 he published his debut collection of poems and stories, *The Suburban*, with Burning Eye Books.

Nadine Rose Johnson – Understudy (Juliet/Miss Capulet)

Nadine recently played the Artful Dodger/Rosie in the 2023 debut and UK tour of Roy Williams' stage adaptation of *Unexpected Twist*, produced by Royal & Derngate and Children's Theatre Partnership, directed by James Dacre. Nadine contributed to music and lyrics during the productions initial R&D which was included in the show and the published play text.

Other theatre credits include *Wishmas* (Secret Cinema); *Arrivals* (imPossible Producing); *Frankenstein: How to Make a Monster* (Battersea Arts Centre); *The Last Man* (Battersea Arts Centre); *#50Days* (Turbine Theatre); *Let's Get Together* (Cardboard Citizens).

Television credits include *Frankenstein: How to Make a Monster* (BBC).

Commercial credits include *Zinger Popcorn Chicken* (KFC) and *Christmas* (McDonalds).

Aminita Francis – Understudy (Capulet/Multi-rolling)

Aminita played the lead role of Henrietta Lacks in the Actors Touring Company production of *Family Tree* directed by Matthew Xia, for which she received nominations for an Offie award for Lead Performance in a Play and for Best Female Lead Actor in a Play – Black British Theatre Awards 2023.

Other theatre credits include *Cinderella* and *Red Riding Hood* (Liverpool Everyman); *I am Kevin* and *Babel* (Wildworks); *Frankenstein: How to Make a Monster* (Battersea Arts Centre); *The Immersive Great Gatsby* (Hartshorn-Hook Productions); *Josephine* (Theatre Royal Bath); *Bugsy Malone* (Lyric Hammersmith); *Afroabelhas Brasil* (British Council/Tempo Festival); *Chocolate Cake* (Polka Theatre); *Hive City Legacy* (The Roundhouse/Hot Brown Honey); *Six Wives* and *The New Morning* (Theatre Royal Stratford East); *Bite Your Tongue* (Hackney Showroom/Talawa); *Blood Wedding*, *Romeo and Juliet* and *The Arsonists* (The Courtyard Theatre/CTTC); *Next Generation* (Zoonation) and *Cabin Fever* (Theatre503).

Television credits include *Frankenstein: How to Make a Monster* (BBC).

Erin C. Guan – Set and Costume Designer

Erin is a London-based scenographer and interactive installation artist from China. Her work spans intercultural performances and minority voices. Her recent theatre projects include *Turandot* (The Opera Makers & Ellandar x Arcola Theatre); *Pied Piper* (Battersea Arts Centre); *The Apology* (New Earth Theatre x Arcola Theatre); *A Gig for Ghost* (Forty Five North x Soho Theatre Upstairs); *Pressure Drop* (Immediate Theatre); *Unchain Me* (Dreamthinkspeak x Brighton Festival); *Prayer for the Hungry Ghost* (Barbican Open Lab); *Foxes* (Defibrillator Theatre x Theatre503); *Tokyo Rose* (Burnt Lemon Theatre); both immersive game theatre *Talk* and *The House Never Wins* (Kill The Cat Theatre). Her recent TV work includes costume design for *East Mode S2* with Nigel Ng (Comedy Central x Channel 5).

Jonathan Chan – Lighting Designer

Jonathan trained at the Guildhall School of Music and Drama. His credits include *Ignition* (Frantic Assembly); *The Flea* (Yard Theatre); *Kim's Convenience, Candy* (Park Theatre); *Love Bomb* (NYT); *Duck* (Arcola Theatre); *Grindr: The Opera* (Union Theatre); *Snowflakes* (Park Theatre and Old Red Lion Theatre Pub); *In the Net* (Jermyn Street); *Grandad, Me and Teddy Too* (Polka Theatre); *Tiny Tim's Christmas Carol, She Stoops to Conquer, The Solid Life of Sugar Water* (Orange Tree Theatre); *Lady Dealer* (Paines Plough Roundabout); *An Interrogation* (Summerhall); *Move Fast and Break Things* (Camden People's and Summerhall); *Pussycat in Memory of Darkness, The Straw Chair* (Finborough Theatre); *Maybe Probably, Belvedere* (Old Red Lion Pub Theatre); *Different Owners at Sunrise* (The Roundhouse); *Urinetown: the Musical, Opera Makers* (Guildhall); *Fidelio* (Glyndebourne – Assistant Lighting Designer) and *The Passenger R&D* (Guildhall – Associate Lighting Designer).

Simon Beyer – Sound Designer and Stage Manager

Simon is a freelance theatre maker, working both in the creative side as a director, writer, composer, and sound and lighting designer, and the practical side as a producer, production manager and technical/stage manager. Theatre credits include *When the Lilac Blooms My Love* (Leicester Square Theatre as director); *My Fifteen Minutes The Musical* (New Wimbledon Studio as writer/director); *The Werewolf of Washington Heights* (Cockpit Theatre as sound/lighting designer); *Ghosts in the Attic* (Brockley Jack Studio as writer/director); *Iphigenia* (New Diorama Theatre as composer/lighting designer); *Studies For A Portrait* (White Bear Theatre and transfer to Oval House as producer); *Tales of Gin and Tonic* (Playground Theatre as producer); *A Critical Stage* (Tabard Theatre as lighting designer); *Love and Destruction: One Man* (Playground Theatre as lighting/sound designer);

The Tempest (The Cock Tavern Theatre as director/ composer).

Technical, stage and production management credits include *Plastic Drastic Fantastic* (Akademi UK tour); *Measure for Measure* (Drayton Arms Theatre); *The Good Dad* (Golden Goose Theatre); *Scotch Egg Musical* (Drayton Arms Theatre and transfer to The Playground Theatre).

He is currently artistic director of Paper Breadcrumbs Production Company and former roles include executive producer and founder of The Cock Tavern Theatre, chair of the board of trustees for Stone Crabs Theatre Company, general manager at The Playground Theatre, producer for Good Night Out Presents and artistic director for the Ant Theatre Company.

About Polka Theatre

Polka is the home of children's theatre.

Polka opened its doors in 1979 and was the UK's first theatre venue dedicated exclusively to children. Still only one of just a handful of dedicated children's venues in the UK, the venue re-opened in 2021 after a state-of-the-art major renovation and presents a year-round programme of shows and creative learning activities for ages 0–12.

With two theatre spaces, a rehearsal/community space, a Clore Learning Studio, a café, an outdoor play area and garden and exhibition spaces, Polka is unique in its child-centred design, and is open all year round as a creative community hub in the Merton borough. The theatre is known for the high production values of theatre for young audiences, an expansive and innovative Creative Learning programme, and the exceptional environment in which these are produced.

Importantly, Polka also provides a permanent London venue for touring children's theatre companies from all over the UK and abroad.

About Beats & Elements

Beats & Elements was started in 2013 by Paul Cree and Conrad Murray, with the aim to create hip hop theatre, and fuse their passion of music, rap and theatre. They also had a joint passion for young people and created a workshop practice that they used in schools, community centres, universities and drama schools.

They aimed to create powerful theatre, using beats, beatbox, loopers, synths, guitars and spoken word. They had the aim of telling untold stories, and platforming new artists and artforms.

They were supported by Camden People Theatre and created the hit show *No Milk for the Foxes*. They used the show to hold post show gigs to platform artists they were excited about. One of these artists was Lakeisha Lynch-Stevens.

In around 2016, they asked Lakeisha and rapper/performer Gambit Ace to join the company to create *High Rise eState Of Mind* for Camden People's Theatre and Battersea Arts Centre. It was a powerful show which addressed the UK Housing issue.

'lively, likeable quartet of performers.' **** The Stage

'musical talent in bucketloads.' Everything Theatre

They continue to create music and theatre, and work in some of the UK top drama schools including Exeter University, Goldsmiths, LAMDA, Central, Mountview and Fourth Monkey.

Beats & Elements: A Hip Hop Theatre Trilogy was published by Methuen Drama in 2022.

Romeo and Juliet: A Hip Hop Adaptation

By Katie Beswick

The tradition of adaptation – which means taking one version of a story and retelling it in a new form – is older than literature itself. As soon as humans began to tell stories to one another, we also retold those stories; making them our own or offering a new spin on something very familiar. Many of Shakespeare's plays were, in fact, adaptations of older works, or references to existing literature, including *Romeo and Juliet*. Arthur Brooke's poem, 'The Tragicall Historye of Romeus and Juliet' is understood to have been an important source for Shakespeare's play. To further illustrate the point, Brooke's work was also an adaptation – he'd used a translation of a story in Italian writer Matteo Bandello's *Novelle* as inspiration for his verse. There is, it turns out, nothing new under the sun.

This cycle of translation and adaptation is continued in this Polka Theatre/Beats & Elements adaptation of *Romeo and Juliet*. Here, as you will see, elements of the famous play are recycled into a modern-day street tale – familiar characters become new people; Shakespeare's words are flipped and reused; and settings that we might know from our own lives are rendered on stage. In this version, hip hop is used a means of storytelling. Hip hop is a global culture and practice that emerged from inner city New York in the 1970s; it can be identified by four 'pillars': rapping (or emceeing); b-boying (or breakdancing); graffiti; and deejaying. Hip hop can be seen in the play in lots of ways, from the rap verses to the movement – but it's also there in the style of the telling, which uses the theatre-makers' experience of south-west London as a lens with which to explore Shakespeare's themes. This use of lived experience might be understood within a hip hop frame too: the concept of 'knowledge' is often positioned as hip hop's fifth 'pillar' and refers to the way hip hop culture enables a sharing of knowledge from one person to another, as well as to a deep spiritual sense of knowledge and connection which many hip hop fans share.

If you are studying English Literature, the technique of reworking, referencing and retelling is sometimes known as 'intertextuality' – which means the ways different texts relate to one another. In hip hop, adaptation and the use of referencing is known as 'sampling' (taking words or phrases and reusing them), and 'remixing' (making an existing thing new by changing it). There are many reasons why we might sample and remix – to pay homage to the original; to bring our own personalities to a famous work; to show the relevance of a historical story to the present day; to improve on what has gone before; or to make our audiences laugh. Throughout this version of *Romeo and Juliet* there are references not only to the original, but to other cultural works and familiar phrases and images that help the play to feel modern and located in its Merton setting.

What words, phrases, ideas and images can you find in the play that refer to other things? How do these make you feel? Why do you think the theatre makers have chosen to use them in this adaptation? Answering these questions might help you to understand the show more deeply, or to find levels of meaning that aren't obvious straight away.

Romeo and Juliet

Characters

Romeo, *the son of the current Lord and Lady Montague*
Juliet, *the daughter of the current Lord and Lady Capulet*
Mercutio, *Romeo's best friend*
Tybalt, *Juliet's cousin, the 'Sergeant Major' for the Capulets out in the streets of Merton*
Freddy, *the manager of Merton's Community Centre. Staff of two but still manages to welcome and support whoever comes. He is easily spoken over.*
Paris, *Juliet's arranged suitor*
Benvolio, *one of Merton's finest Police Community Support Officers (PCSO)*
Capulet, *father of* **Juliet**
Lady Capulet, *mother of* **Juliet**, *wife of* **Capulet**

Capulets *are dressed in street wear, think Adidas and Run DMC, and the* **Montagues** *are dressed in ruffles, as imagined were worn in Shakespearean times.*

Merton, 2024

Scene One

Star-Crossed Lovers

(Choral singing.)

Actor 1

Two households, both alike in dignity,
In fair Verona,

All

Merton!

Actor 1

Merton, where we lay our scene.
From ancient grudge break to new mutiny,
Where civil blood makes civil hands unclean.

(Chords – F, G, Bb, DM) Hip hop beatbox.

All

Found one another,
Star-crossed lovers,
It wasn't meant to be.
Can't be together,
Love undercover,
Love is all they need.
A rose by any other name.
Found one another,
Star-crossed lovers,
It wasn't meant to be.

Two postcodes, two streets apart
In dear Merton where our story starts.

Actor 2

Beef from the past creates new tension.
Innocent blood spilled, they need an intervention.

Actor 3

A boy and a girl, supposed to be ops;
They chat, hold hands, secret meetings by the shops.

Actor 4

But these link ups are lamented, their lives are suspended:
Fam devastated but at least their war is ended.

Actor 1

These two young youts who were really in love,
Their parents fighting, feuding, fuming, all of the above,

Actor 2

Nothing could have stopped it, but the giving of their
hearts.
Welcome to this story and all of its parts.

Actor 3

If you wanna know the T then just lend us your ears;
We'll sing and rap and rhyme, it'll all become clear.

(*Sung.*)

Found one another,
Star-crossed lovers,
It wasn't to be.

Can't be together,
Love undercover,
Love is all they need.

A rose by any other name.

Found one another,
Star-crossed lovers,
It wasn't meant to be.

Scene Two

Say Hello to the Characters

We're introduced to the people of Merton.

(*Chords – E, G*) *Hip hop beatbox.*

All
> Bringing the story the death and glory
> And leaving it on the stage
> The tale of Romeo and Juliet, Romeo and Juliet

Benvolio
> Oh, I'm Benvolio, I really can't stay here for too long, I've gotta go
> I volunteer on the city streets
> Officially – since March of last year – been a police
>
> It's easy to stress
> And yes I've seen death
> My Montague family name's rep – is really not the best but I can say truly
> Since the thing last year that I'm a new me

Capulet
> I'm CEO Capulet
> Owner of property
> Houses to let
> Juliet's my girl
> I'll give her anything in this whole damned world
> We hate the Montagues
> But they choose
> To carry on this war
> So of course
> We crush them
> At any chance
> We come first
> They come last

Mercutio
> What you saying? I'm Mercutio.
> I guess that you should know
> I'm always rolling with my bro

Mercutio *and* **Romeo**
> But I do have other homies though
>
> You can find me with the Montagues
> Roll up on the wrong side of the Manor and I promise you

Pop blap – make you wanna run back
Have to get the strap when you're dealing with them Caps

Tybalt

I'm Tybalt
I'm vexed all time
And it ain't my fault
I gotta watch my cousin's moves
She's going on mad
Going on rude
I'm working these streets for my uncle
Most other families have gone under
We're on bitcoin FTSE 100
Cash money, trust funded

Freddy

I'm Freddy, I know some of you would be familiar already
If you've grown up anywhere around my home
Merton's own, I run the Community Centre on my own
In the old days we would play CDs, now it's tablets, games
and flat TVs

Paris

I'm Paris
Friend of the Capulets
Down with Daddy
Juliet's mine
We're gonna get married
Ow she's a baddie!
I'll teach her respect
We'll go to Dubai
And fly on jets.
She just needs to learn to listen
This Sunday is our wedding.

All

Bringing the story, the death and glory
And leaving it on the stage
The tale of Romeo and Juliet, Romeo and Juliet

Romeo

    Name's Romeo
    The golden boy Montague
    All my life I've been tangled in this curséd feud
    I was born into this hate not many can relate
    I just want to live and love in this unhappy place

(*Sung.*)

    I found my wife amongst my enemies
    In her arms I've got everything I need
    Our families won't let us be
    Will we ever find peace you'll have to wait and see

Juliet

    I'm a Capulet, mainly I'm Juliet
    The one from the title, head to head and rival
    Of the Montagues. Don't get me, I didn't choose.
    Dad runs the street from that bin there to where
    Broadway meets Merton High Street
    Cousin Tybalt is as close as a brother, but he acts
    something other when he sees a Montague,
    tryna to keep him calm so he lives past thirty-two

All

    Bringing the story the death and glory
    And leaving it on the stage
    The tale of Romeo and Juliet, Romeo and Juliet

    Bringing the story the death and glory
    And leaving it on the stage
    The tale of Romeo and Juliet, Romeo and Juliet

Scene Three

The Capulet Cotch

A **Capulet** *and a* **Montague** *come across each other on* **Capulet** *cotch, just off from Montague Manor.*

(*Chord E*)

Capulet
Do you kiss your teeth fam?

Montague
Nah fam

Capulet
You kissed your teeth man!

Montague
Yes I kiss my teeth man!

Capulet
Do you kiss your teeth at me fam?

Montague
You fam? Nah fam!

Capulet
Are you sure fam?

Montague
What you saying man?

Capulet
Are you beefing man?

Montague
What you saying if I am fam?

Capulet
What I'm saying is you don't belong fam.
Can't come onto streets like you own it – Damn –
Shoulda took it when you had the chance man, teefing
everything else, like you did back then! Huh?

Montague
You think we took everything from you,
Playing the victim, yeh sounds like you!
What d'you hate us more for? Take your pick
We only got your money coz your family's thick.

Capulet
Ah you went too far man, you're taking the mick

Montague
Don't care, you Capulets make me sick

Capulet
I'd rather be a Capulet than Montague scum
Mont – You better get ready to die, your days are done

Benvolio
Stop your fighting!
Get your arse home!
Ain't nothing you can say that's worth dying for
Fools

Scene Four

He Wants to be a Capulet

Capulet *and* **Lady Capulet** *discuss* **Paris'** *wishes to marry their daughter,* **Juliet.**

Hip hop beatbox.

Capulet
Honey, last night that nice young guy Paris
Managed to catch me for quite a serious chat,
And of course we had a little back and forth
And after a while he put forth his real cause

Lady Capulet
Babes, can we just pause right there
Hold that thought right there
Look I'm totally aware
That he's always hanging around, and it's like he's *always*
there.
But what about Juliet?

Capulet
He wants to get married
He's in a hurry
I can see him at our daughter's side

He's a nice guy
I know this is right

He wants to be a Capulet
Who wouldn't want to be a Capulet?
WE run this city
We run this town
We run this city,
We run this town!

He asked me for her hand
And I was really gassed
That he would that
A *real* man!
And then he called me Dad!
I felt really proud
Invited him to the house.

Lady Capulet
Darling our dear daughter oughta be consulted first?
Did that thought cross your mind berk?
You know that she worships you,
And your every word
Do you think that this can work?

Capulet
She's gonna wed Paris
And they will be happy
I want the best for my girl
He'll join the company
It's gonna work, you'll see!

He wants to be a Capulet
Who wouldn't want to be a Capulet?
WE run this city
We run this town
We run this city,
We run this town!

Scene Five

Walking Down the Aisle

Capulet *and* **Juliet** *discuss* **Juliet***'s future; the wedding day they've*
always dreamed of.

(Chords – Verse D, G, A, D. Bridge G, A, D) Gentle, ballad.

Capulet
Juliet, since you were knee high
You've been the special girl by my side
But pretty soon you'll be another guy's
When I walk you down the aisle
It brings a tear to my eye

Juliet
Hey Dad, you're making me die
You're cracking me up
I got a pain in my side
Even when I leave,
It will never be bye
When you walk me down the aisle
It brings a tear to my eye

Capulet
And when that day finally comes
I'll cry a million tears
And when tomorrow
Finally comes
We will wonder what happened to our years

Juliet
Hey Dad, I promise you
I'll do anything you ask me to
And best believe I'm ever ruled by you
When I'm walking down the aisle
I'll give you a little smile

Scene Six

Take it Slow (Montague Manor)

An invite comes in for a house party at **Tybalt***'s house.* **Mercutio** *tries to convince his best friend* **Romeo** *to go along with him, as* **Rosalind** *–* **Romeo***'s ex – will be there.*

(Chords – C, D, G, Em) Hip hop beatbox.

All
Take it slow Romeo
Sometimes, you will learn,
Fools rush in.

Romeo
Look, I told you before man, me and her are done

Mercutio
You told me last week, Rosalind was the one!

Romeo
I was out of my mind; I weren't thinking straight!
Plus she texts love hearts everyday

Mercutio
Ah mate
I swear when you were with Kim in Year 8
You were moaning for days, all pressed cos her texts were delayed
Weeks would go by and you hadn't heard a thing

Romeo
Ay bruv, bun Kim – she broke my heart by the swing
But at least she was leng, Rosalind's kinda dead
Her breath stinks and she's got this weird dent in her head

Mercutio
It's called her brain, that girl's going uni man Ro
She loves history like Bridgerton all that stuff you don't know

Romeo
That stuff sounds kinda sick –

Mercutio
See you and her, you just fit!

Romeo
She still gives me the ick

Mercutio
Ahh you're taking the mick
Her parents are rich – plus they're young and they're hip
What other forty-year-old is gonna buy you this drip
They bought her driving lessons

Romeo
What? Are you sure that's legit?

Mercutio
Bruv in three years' time she'll be driving a whip

Romeo
Bro I've heard enough, I don't care about a whip
Me and that girl are through – you can tell her I quit

All
Take it slow Romeo
Sometimes you'll learn
Fools rush in

Mercutio
I got a text

Romeo
From who?

Mercutio
The Capulets

Romeo
Say less

Mercutio
Nah bro, hear me out!

Romeo

No way that's dread
Been fighting for years, now I'm the young head
If they see me on road, then blood will be shed

Mercutio

They're only there on party vibes
Not like that time when we got rushed when we were on
our bikes
The Montagues, me and you – cycling side by side
You know I'll always have your back, you know I'm down
to ride
I'm not saying let's move mad but I'm not tryna hide
Biggest party of the year, of course we're gonna slide
Man I'm on a hype, we're both gonna be rolling there –
facts
Even if I have to chase you up or drag you on my back

Romeo

Bro relax
Sometimes I feel like I'm stuck in a trap
Capulets on every corner
Stressed out I can't lack
But today I'm done hiding
Now I'm on the attack
I'ma show em who's the boss
Knowing you got my back
Cos me and you been through it all
And we still stand tall
And cos you've never let me down
I'll always answer your call
So let's go to this party bro let's both catch a vibe
Ain't no Capulet Fools gonna ruin our night

All

Take it slow Romeo
Sometimes, you will learn,
Fools rush in.

Scene Seven

House Party

Loop station track. **Juliet***'s letting loose having fun at* **Tybalt***'s party – she's interrupted by* **Tybalt** *who's annoyed and confused as to why* **Paris** *hasn't been invited.*

House loop – loopstation.

Juliet
  Have a good time
  Sip a little wine
  Coke and lime
  And just chill out

Tybalt *pulls* **Juliet** *out of the crowd –*

Tybalt
  Where's Paris?
  You were told to tell him 'bout the party,
  But you haven't
  I asked him if he knew
  And you said you text him,
  But it turns out that now you didn't

Juliet
  Tybalt, my cuz, I love you, but
  It's not up to me to invite your mate
  He's sweet and all that, but he's beggin', like wait.
  I've known him for years, he's like a brother,
  Thanks for the set-up, but I wanna find another.

Tybalt
  Listen!
  You're way too hood
  For man like P
  He's too good, big player in the game
  You're lucky he even knows your name

Juliet

Don't watch that!

Have a good time
Sip a little wine
Coke and lime
And just chill out

Romeo *is feeling uneasy, being surrounded by Capulets,* **Mercutio**
tries to reassure him.

Mercutio

That's Rosalind's friend over there
So she should be somewhere over here
I think I deeped her near by the stairs
I swear that, that's her sister on the chairs

Romeo

Nah man I'm feeling proper scared
All these people, I feel the stares
Something evil, up in the air
Think I'm gonna get out of here

Mercutio

Don't fear – we rolled here as a two
The Capulets are mad but what are they gonna do
Rosalind is back, she's just come from the loos
She's tryna dry her hands while she's looking at you

Romeo

I swear bro you ain't listening
Stepped to the opps now the beef's all sizzling
Tybalt's crazy he stays strapped up
I don't wanna be here when the ting starts whistling
So I'm cutting right now plus that chick ain't perfect
Rosalinds like a two-out-of-ten she ain't worth it
I need me a wife wid a body that's cursive
Wait who's that in the back just lurking
who's that chick?

Mercutio
She's a Capulet, bro – are you thick?

Romeo
Who's that chick?

Mercutio
Ah mate – you're taking the mick

Romeo
Who's that chick?

Mercutio
Rosalind can see us bro – you need to get a grip

Romeo
Who's that chick? Nah gimme a minute man, I'll make this quick

Romeo Montague *and* **Juliet Capulet** *meet, it's love at first sight.*

Romeo
Excuse me
What's your name
I ain't seen no one as leng as you before.

Juliet
My name?
You gotta work for that
I haven't seen you before
How is that?

Romeo
Don't watch that
I'm outside tho
I'm getting money
Filling banks like a silo
I gotta dip but your eyes kinda sweet
Put your name in my phone
Better not be a typo

Juliet
Sure of yourself, that you're gonna get my number
You ain't got my name yet,

Starts with a J and ends with an -et
You earned that much off your 'sweet eyes' comment
Now looking at you, you're tryin' right?
You got a nice smile and your garms are tight
But looking at your shape up that's not right.
Your face a bit sweaty, I'm still looking for your height.

Romeo

Damn: that's ice cold
You got a sharp tongue
Killed a couple man, but you came for the wrong one
Smile nice and your frame is so petite
Funny that you act hard when you're red in your cheek
I know you're feeling the kid you can't hide it
About my height though
Don't lie girl, you know that you like it
You want a real man, I know girl I'm psychic
And you're a real woman so
Stop being childish

Juliet

Ay you're smart and you know it, but I don't mind it
See you're sharp with words and I got a mind to match
that
Felt trapped that
Every man that
Got close was a doormat,
No chat back.

Romeo

I can't lie you been dealing wid some lames
Greek god Adonis man I'm in my own lane
But suttin 'bout you I can tell that your special
Seen good girls before
But you're on another level

Juliet

You're not bad you know you're passing the test
But I'm not always good

Romeo

Nah you're better than the rest

Juliet

I'll admit there's a little bit of red in my cheek,
(*Aside.*)
If he says something else, then my knees'll go weak
That's peak, talking Greek, I can't speak!
He's on streak. Shut up!
(*To* **Romeo**.)
You could be my type, might swipe right
I'm feeling you fine,

Romeo

So you better be mine?

Wait, I see a Capulet
I swear down that's a Capulet
I'm getting scared that's a Capulet
I only feel this fear round the Capulets

Now it's clear to see
Tybalt bussin the corner coming straight to me
Time running out I ain't finished yet
But if I stay I'm getting capped by a Capulet
This drama's getting peak
Found a new love. This girl so sweet but
Beef's on grill if I stay I'm mince meat
So I've got no choice
Have to make a retreat
Wait what's your name?

Juliet

Juliet Capulet

Romeo

What?

Juliet

Juliet

Mercutio
Capulet!

Tybalt *kisses teeth*.

Mercutio
Did you kiss your teeth fam?!

Tybalt
That's a Montague!
What's wrong with you?
You're so dumb
I'm so done with you!
I'm get my boys to kick him up,
Stick him up,
Hit him up!

Juliet
Don't watch that

Have a good time
Sip a little wine
Coke and lime
Chill out chill out x2

How is that fair, that the one guy there with the sick black
hair and a brain that ain't air
Has to be team Montague,
Couldn't see it in front of you?!

Have a good time
Sip a little wine
Bump and grind

Scene Eight

Juliet's Block 1

Romeo *FaceTimes* **Juliet**.

(*Chords – Dmaj7*) *R&B beatbox*.

Romeo
Say yeahhhh yeah yeah yeahiiyeaghhhh

Say yeahhhh yeah yeah yeahiiyeaghhhh

My Juliet (*Low.*)
My Juliet (*Low.*)
My Juliet (*High.*)
My Juliet (*High.*)

J U L I E T

J U L I E T

J U L I E T

J U L I E T

(*Riff on* **Juliet.**)

Romeo
Bro bro I got it

Mercutio
Her number?

Romeo
No / what? no her Insta bro

Mercutio
What?

Romeo
Juliet's –

Mercutio
No

Romeo
I think I'm in love

Mercutio
She didn't give you her number

Romeo
So? I'm still on her. She's / bad

Mercutio
Mad

Romeo
I'm gonna call her

Mercutio
You're moving like a stalker
Plus don't forget – you had to search up Juliet Capulet

Romeo
I know that she's a Capulet
That's factually accurate
But I can't get her off my mind
So now I'm belling off her line

FaceTime ringing sfx / Pick up sfx.

Juliet
Romeo Montague,
Is that really you?
Romeo, Romeo,
Is that all there is to you?

I see so much more.
That smile, those eyes, oh they hypnotise.
If you said you loved me, I'd shiver
I'd throw my name into the river.

Romeo –

Romeo
Yes?

Juliet
How d'you get my number?

Romeo
Might have stalked your Insta . . .?

Juliet
Kind of weird but I like it
Romeo!

Romeo

My Juliet!
I'm being honest, I know you're a Capulet
The truth is I was born a Montague
But tonight I know that I was made for you

Juliet

Oh Romeo,
I don't mind you're a Montague,
But you better watch your back for what my cousin might
do to you

Romeo

He can bring a thousand straps
Crucify me beat me blue and black
It don't matter what they do to me
Because when I'm in your arms I'm free.
And I can see the moon is jealous of your eyes it's true
Sunlight glistens on your skin favour morning dew
My family's broken, so is yours
Together we're the glue
I'll walk through fire
If it means I get to be with you

Juliet

That's romantic,
Never heard it before
My mates are fun, but they have never heard of metaphor
Don't act all hard and that
My cousin can't be messed with,
I've seen him pushing grannies, throwing bricks and
nicking Teslas

Romeo

Look I'm no longer afraid

Juliet

There's no way out no escape

Romeo
Hold my hand let's be brave
Cos together we're safe

Juliet
Romeo!

Romeo
Juliet

Romeo *and* **Juliet**
Is that really you?

Juliet
Romeo!

Romeo
My Juliet

Romeo *and* **Juliet**
I'm whole now I've found you

Scene Nine

Freddy (The Community Centre – Freddy's Palace)

Freddy's welcomes everyone to Merton's Community Centre. **Romeo**
arrives for some advice. **Freddy** *agrees to help him, inspired by the*
prospect of this bringing peace to Merton.

(Chords – E7#9) Bluesy rock.

Freddy
Grab on, buckle your seat
If you've moved to Merton then you've moved in with me
Your guide, we're going full speed
Touring won't be boring around the Community
Centre

Freddy
Freddy!

All
Freddy, Freddy!

Freddy
Your friend Freddy!

All
Freddy, Freddy!

Freddy
I'm your friend Freddy!

All
Freddy, Freddy!

Freddy
Your friend Freddy!

All
Freddy, Freddy!

Freddy
The things I've seen, you could only dream,
My friends are foes, all buy the things I grow,
Call up, my number's free
I could never have you out here lost in the streets
'Cause I'm
Freddy!

All
Freddy, Freddy!

Freddy
I'm your friend Freddy!

All
Freddy, Freddy!

Freddy
You can count on me friend Freddy!

All
Freddy, Freddy!

Freddy

Mother F –

Romeo

Freddy!

Can you help me (Freddy)?

R&B beatbox.

Romeo

So look I
Met this girl last night
Man we caught a vibe
When I looked into her eyes
Felt like the stars aligned
But then my enemies arrived
Had to take flight
And that's when I realised
That we're on opposing sides
But I still wanna make her mine
Feel like God have me a sign
I ain't never felt this way before
Want her to be my wife

So

Can you help me out Freddy
I really need some help Freddy
I need some real advice Freddy
Want her to be my wife Freddy

Freddy

Romeo that's amazing
Since the age of two I've been waiting
To see a love that's truly captivating
I believe in you and you've made me
So much more
Embracing
In a world of Juliets, I'm changing

I can do you a deal on a cheap ring
But never father the kids cos she'll take them

I mean Romeo ignore me
I'm thinking of dudes who came before me
Aren't you sick of the feuds and all the warring?
This girl and you could be important
More than Merton thought of
You Montagues can get caught up
Always on the news and reports
When Capulets they never get caught
This could bring peace and more
Your Freddy votes all for
I'll be your priest in war
I've been ordained before
This could end beef for all
Imagine a Merton that's peaceful

Romeo

You really get ordained online?

Freddy

Yeah, www dot get-ordained-really-quickly-without-
waiting-too-long dot com

Scene Ten

I Should be the One

R&B drill.

Paris *is hanging around outside* **Juliet***'s block, she interrupts his*
thoughts. He reminds her that the **Capulets** *would prefer her to be*
with him.

Paris

Girl you know I'm gonna be the one
Who was there, when it's all said and done?
You know me and your fam get along
You don't deserve these other guys

To be doing you wrong
I known you for most of your life
I've seen it all
Call me mister dependable
Don't throw my love away
Tomorrow will be yesterday
You know you belong to me
I can't wait much more

Juliet

Is that Romeo?

Paris

No Juliet it's me

Juliet

I'm so sorry course it is! It's late. Err . . . Do you wanna
come in?

Paris

– NO, only if you want me to

Juliet

What do you want, it's late it's like you're in a mood

Paris

The Capulets really wants me with you
Your old man said
I could join the company too

Juliet

Where did you hear this?

Paris

Well I just heard this right now

Juliet

Why did you only just say?

Paris

– Because I only just heard!

Juliet
Tell me every single thing word for word

Paris
I'm too busy

Juliet
What for me?

Paris
Girl you mess with my head!

Juliet
So you and Dad just decided my future tonight
This is messed up

Paris
Look that's what they said!

Girl you know that I could be the one
Who was there, when it's all said and done?
You know me and your fam get along
But you always seem to be feeling these guys
Who are wrong
I known you for most of your life
I've seen it all
Call me mister dependable
Don't throw my love away
Tomorrow will be yesterday
You belong to me
I can't wait much more

Juliet
Paris did you say something?

Paris
Just go to him.

Scene Eleven

Romeo and Juliet Get Married

(Chords – C, Am, F, G) Ballad

Freddy *has been ordained online, he secretly marries* **Romeo** *and* **Juliet** *– in the basement of the Community Centre.*

Romeo (*pause*)
  Exactly

Juliet
  I don't hate it

Romeo
  You look like you wanna smack me
  but I'll take it – know it's not the wedding you deserve
  but I face you – knowing I can't have you in a church
  but a basement, waste of such a beautiful face
  and I pray that we take this one day
  where we're blocking out hate
  where we lock in our fates
  Swear it's you and me against
  the earth
  You were made for me, curse
  all of our enemies
  Hurting and resenting
  You're worth it every second
  The threatens of cars going past
  Smashes I can hear and the alarms
  Officers armed, (*To* **Freddy**.) the door locked yeah?

Juliet
  / Stay calm

Freddy
  Stay calm, stay calm, it's not a clip from a drama
  Well it is a bit of a disaster but you also get a wife and you
  live forever after.
  Romeo, will you take this ring?

Romeo
I do

Freddy
Say to Juliet – you'll give her everything

Romeo
Yes I do

Freddy
Say I vow to everything

Romeo
I do

Freddy
/ I vow to everything

Romeo
I vow to everything

Freddy
Ha! Ordained!
I mean can you both sign each other's names?
You didn't say if your surnames were gonna change
Or stay the same – none of my business though, I'm not complaining
I was actually gonna say but in this day and age
Ask an innocent question and it's on the front page
But it's kinda contagious
Just wanting some tea
But it's both of your days
Not this old fool's, don't mind me
Rightfully light leads when there's darkness
What do you see without this partner?

Romeo
Nothing

Juliet
Pain

Romeo
Would matter

Juliet
Same

Freddy
You put us to shame – you young ones have mastered
the age of block and delete and carve out your own path
The art of
Following your hearts
When taking chances
Is a bit of a disaster – (*To* **Juliet**.) it's alright you get a whole
hubby and you live forever after
Juliet, will you take this ring?

Juliet
I do

Freddy
Say to Romeo – you'll give him everything

Juliet
Yes I do

Freddy
Will you really vow to everything?

Julie
I do.

Freddy
Say / I vow to everything

Julie
I vow to everything

Scene Twelve

No Man's Pleasure (Montague Theme)

Hip hop beatbox.

Mercutio *is wound up – tensions between the Capulets and the*
Montagues are rising – **Mercutio** *wants the Capulets to know he*
won't be messed with.

Mercutio

Tybalt kissed his teeth fam!

I will not budge, for no man's pleasure
I jump onto the Tube, see all commuters start to tremble
They offer me their seats, then Romeo tells me to settle
I don't care if you're old or if you're homeless – I'm a rebel

Romeo

No you're not – you're a lot
Well a lot of noise
Especially when we're tryna avoid –

Mercutio

What? Me chilling with my boy?

Romeo

You know the cost –

Mercutio

You lost your voice?
If they want it then that's their choice
Done nothing but just be boys

Romeo *and* **Mercutio**

I will not budge, for no man's pleasure

Mercutio

/ The Montagues they call me when they need someone to
settle

Romeo

We're Montagues of course we're gonna cause the opps to
tremble

Mercutio

That Tybalt lights a fuse in me, he thinks he's on my level
I find it so amusing, guess he thinks his cousin's special

Romeo

Mercoosh, don't be so rude

Mercutio

I said what I said
You're a Montague act like it
Coming at me for Capulets

I will not budge, for no man's pleasure
Remember back when we were younger and I said I'd ask
no questions
If you call me under pressure that I'd be there in a second
That's a blessing, future best man and your friend –

Romeo

Yeah you're the best

Mercutio

Say I will not budge, I will not budge,
/ I will not budge for no man

Romeo

I will not budge, for no man's pleasure
/ We're Montagues of course we're gonna cause the opps
to tremble

Mercutio

Say I will not budge, for no man
/ Say I will not budge, for no man

Romeo

I will not budge, for no man's pleasure
/ We're Montagues of course we're gonna cause the opps
to tremble
I will not budge, for no man's pleasure

Mercutio

/ Say I will not budge, for no man
I will not budge, for no man's pleasure

Scene Thirteen

Mercutio Death

Hip hop beatbox.

Mercutio *and* **Tybalt** *get into an encounter,* **Mercutio** *is killed.*

Mercutio
Tybalt!

Tybalt
Mercutio

Mercutio
What you looking at yo?

Tybalt
I weren't looking at you bro.

Mercutio
You think you're bad?

Tybalt
Have you gone delulu?

Mercutio
Take this

Mercutio *swings for* **Tybalt**.

Tybalt
You missed!
I didn't wanna do you

Tybalt *swings bat at* **Mercutio**.

Mercutio
That was a scratch

Tybalt
Ha!

Tybalt *swings bat, hitting* **Mercutio** *hard.*

Mercutio
That'll leave a bruise

Tybalt *swings and hits again hard.*

Tybalt
Ha!

Mercutio
That'll take some healing

Mercutio *leaves in a hurry, head pouring with blood.* **Juliet**'s *on the phone.*

Juliet
Yo ben, what's the message?
Mercutio's in the hospital bleeding!
He's NOT breathing!

Scene Fourteen

Romeo's on the Run

Hip hop beatbox.

Romeo *kills* **Tybalt** *in self-defence. He's banished.*

Benvolio
Romeo Romeo,
Mercutio murked
I don't wanna see you hurt
You feet digging up the dirt!
Here comes Tybalt back again

Romeo
Again in triumph?
With Mercutio slain?
I'ma send him to heaven
With a power the opposite of that place
Come on cousin
I know your chatting breeze
I can see your lips running !

Tybalt
>Stupid little Gen Z
>You can't mess with me
>This ain't no beef on TikTok
>You about to get a nasty shock

Benvolio
>Tybalt swings with the bat
>But Romeo pops him with the gat
>But the bullets seem to glance his chest
>What's the chances
>One of Verona's beast
>A Capulet cousin
>Sustains the pain
>Of the hot projectile?
>He looks Romeo in the face
>Gives a little smile
>For a second maybe
>Brotherly love?
>Before Tybalt crouches down
>In a pool of his own blood

Romeo
>Where should I run
>Where should I go?
>Why did I do this?
>I don't know

Benvolio
>If you don't leave ends
>It will be your fatal end
>Don't underestimate your foes
>You won't even know your friends.

Romeo
>Why did I do this
>I'm a fool
>Why did I do this
>This is so dumb
>Why did I do this?

Benvolio

Romeo is on the run.

Scene Sixteen

Nobody Can Believe

(*Chords – C, D*)

All

Nobody can believe
It's hard to explain
The man with so much rage
Tybalt Capulet has been slain

Scene Seventeen

Go Easy

(*Chords – F, C*) *Slow ballad beatbox.*

Romeo *hides out at the Community Centre, with the help of*
Freddy.

Romeo

Freddy I was hoping
The Community Centre was open
I didn't know who else to go to

You're a truly a mentor and role model
I need your help Freddy – hold the door
I need to hide

Somewhere inside

Freddy

I've seen some things online

Romeo

It was his life or mine

Freddy I'm hoping you'd let me
Keep my head low in here
Where no one can get me

Freddy

Well I know that you're wanted by police
But now I can't let you walk the streets

Romeo

Tybalt was threatening me
He swung so I killed him before he could get to me

Freddy

My Romeo, gotta keep this on the low
If they know I've helped you then they'll have me in a
hole
If I went to prison I don't think that I could cope
I pray that they go easy on me
And when this blows, Freddy weren't involved,
Freddy didn't help you because Freddy didn't know
You deserve your pardon and you still have time to grow
I pray that they go easy on me

Don't wanna regret this
Or to end up with a sentence
Mugshot felon
In the news with big letters

'Freddy who was once so well respected . . .
Merton's very own . . .'

Romeo

Freddy I get it, I get it

Freddy

/ My Romeo, gotta keep this on the low
If they know I've helped you then they'll have me in a
hole

Romeo

I know

Freddy *and* **Romeo**
>   If I went to prison I don't think that I could cope
>   I pray that they go easy on me

Freddy
>   And when this blows, Freddy weren't involved,
>   Freddy didn't help you because Freddy didn't know
>   You deserve your pardon and you still have time to grow

Freddy *and* **Romeo**
>   I pray that they go easy on me
>   I pray they go easy

Romeo
>   If I lose Juliet then I don't think that I could cope
>   I pray that they go easy on me

Scene Eighteen

My Cousin

Beatbox. Dark, brooding.

Juliet *ponders* **Romeo**'s *reasoning behind killing* **Tybalt**.

Juliet
>   Nah back it up a second
>
>   It's blowing up on TikTok, Insta, X
>   Snapchat covered in my husband's death threats
>   He killed a best friend, a brother, son, a Capulet
>   Tributes pouring in from people Tybalt never met
>
>   Tybalt my cousin
>   Taught me how to ride a bike
>   First man bar my dad to stand by my side
>   'My ride or die' he said – but did he have it on coming?!
>   Ah man he's my cousin what am I saying?!
>
>   Romeo did it? Romeo's the villain of this story that they're
>   telling, I can't believe it

I know Tybalt, a temper, and an ego and if Romeo shot it was I go or he go.

Will he be banished? Just vanish
From my life completely
I just found him to complete me
I can't breathe right when he's away from me
But now because of him bolt exists as a memory

Should I trust him?
Should I believe in him?
Should I just be happy
It wasn't him?

Send me my Romeo
We can say our final farewell

Scene Nineteen

Moonlight Cabaret

(Chords – Amaj7, E, F#m7, G#m7) Beatbox R&B.

Under all the pressure, **Romeo** *and* **Juliet** *share a brief moment.*

Romeo
    Tonight it's only about us
    Juliet come to me
    You know that you can trust

Romeo *and* **Juliet**
    And they
    While the night away
    Their own Moonlight Cabaret
    Everything so fresh and new
    Doing the things that lovers do

Juliet
    Tonight it's only about us
    Romeo come to me
    I'm so filled up with love

Romeo *and* **Juliet**
And they
While the night away
Their own Moonlight Cabaret
Everything fresh and new
Doing the things that lovers do

Romeo
Look babe stop
I gotta be off

Juliet
Romeo Romeo
Please don't go

Romeo
It's getting pretty mad out there
Freddy said that it is getting pretty bad out there

Juliet
Yeah I heard somebody at the back door

Romeo
What! Babes are you sure?
Look I know that you're shook
But I gotta breeze
Cos the heat on the street is peak
Your whole fam looking for me
Plotting on me
Scheming on me
I'll be back in time
Gotta go to High Barnet

Juliet
That's the end of the Northern Line!

Romeo
Yo babes you know I'll be fine.

Juliet
Last night was all about us

Romeo
Juliet come to me

Juliet
Romeo come to me

Romeo *and* **Juliet**
I know that you feel love

And they
While the night away
Their own Moonlight Cabaret
Everything so fresh and new
Doing the things that lovers do

Scene Twenty

Wedding Time

Hip hop beatbox.

The Capulet pressure continues.

Capulet
It's wedding time!
It's wedding time.

Time's ticking
Juliet's wedding
The event of the year
Nobody will forget it
Hey ho!
You're gonna wed Paris
And you can't say 'No'.

Bottom line, it's time
To get your best shoes shined.
There'll be a meat feast
And plenty of fizzy wine
No expense spared
For this daughter of mine.

Lady Capulet
Darling what if she doesn't want to do this

Capulet
That's ludicrous!
There's nothing new to this
I'm the Capulet CEO
Anything I say must go
And she can't say 'No'.
I gave her anything that she wants
This is the future
That she will get
So in a couple of days
She must say 'Yes'
This is the family way
She will do as I say!

It's wedding time!
It's wedding time.

Time's ticking
Juliet's wedding
The event of the year
Nobody will forget it
Hey ho!
You're gonna wed Paris
And you can't say 'No'.

Scene Twenty-One

Fake Death

(*Chords – Bb, Cm7, GM*)

Juliet *turns to* **Freddy** *for help.*

Juliet
Mum wants me with Paris
I can't breathe
Dad's paid for the marriage
What about me?
Now they've picked a date

While Romeo's escaped
Freddy will you help me run away?

Freddy

Maybe I'm out of my mind
I can help you to hide
Write a post online – 'Juliet has died'
Live a life in disguise
You can't be Paris' bride
If they think that you've died
You can be by Romeo's side

Alright I'll go
On my account to put up a post
Make sure everyone knows
You're a ghost
You should know that the coast
Might be clear
But Juliet beware,
You can't be seen anywhere
Once I post rest in peace Juliet
Know that there
Will be comments up everywhere
Filled with love hearts and doves and prayer
Hand emojis
There won't be
A threat to get married
A lonely little Paris
You'd only have to get to
Romeo while he's banished

Juliet

I'll manage
/ If you help me to hide
Write a post online – 'Juliet has died'

Freddy

And I can help you to hide
Saying 'Juliet has died'

Juliet *and* **Freddy**
  Maybe I'm out of my mind

Juliet
  / If you help me to hide
  I can be by Romeo's side

Freddy
  I can help you to hide
  So you can be by Romeo's side

Scene Twenty-Two

'Nobody can believe'

(*Chords – C, D*)

All
  Nobody can believe
  Just what they've heard
  That beautiful child
  Juliet Capulet has died.

Scene Twenty-Three

When You're Number One

(*Chords – Bm7, C#m7, F#m7*)

Juliet *finally puts herself first, she packs to run away and be with* **Romeo**.

Juliet
  When you're number one

  Oh this is crazy
  My heart is banging like never before
  I'm gonna be at Romeo's door
  I gotta fight a little bit more

If I believe for just a second
I'll see I'm stronger than I thought I was
Oh
People try and control me, but I'll decide who I marry

When you're number one
You'll see that you are someone
Live the life you need fly free

If people love me, they'll look out for me
Want the best, they'll keep me safe
Oh
they won't limit me
They'll say be brave

When you're number one
You'll see that you are someone
Live the life you need fly free

And I really need to trust myself
There's a feeling in my heart and head
Oh I think that this plan could work
So I better go and play dead

When you're number one
You'll see that you are someone
Live the life you need fly free

We can live the life we need
We will fly free

Scene Twenty-Four

Take it Slow, Reprise (North Side Trauma)

(Chords – C, D, G, Em)

Romeo *sees* **Freddy**'s *post announcing* **Juliet**'s *death*.

All
    Take it slow Romeo
    Sometimes, you will learn,
    Fools rush in.

Romeo

I wonder how my dear Juliet sleeps
It feels like years have passed but it's just been a week
I still ain't used to these ends
The north side gives me the creeps
There ain't a Morley's anywhere
What the heck do they eat?

Lately I've been seeing her in my dreams
The last one was hella scary hope it ain't what it seems
She was holding me while I lay dead in her arms
Let me check my phone
That will erase all these scenes

(*Ping.*)

Is it even so?
Is this a flipping lie
Freddy posting that my dear
Juliet has died?
He's chatting wass
I can't believe my eyes
If this is real
I'd rather be in denial
My bride
So divine
Our hearts were intertwined
A gorgeous face
And to match she was so kind
Everyday I thanked God
That she was all mine
And now you've taken her from me?
There ain't a worse crime!

Without her I've got nothing left
Her love was my life
Now it's taken my breath
Till death do us part
I know that's what we said

But if I can't have you by my side
Then I'd rather be dead

Then
I'll take my own life
What good has it been?
Only seen pain and strife
If this is my fate
I won't put up a fight
At last in death
I can be with my wife

All

Take it slow Romeo
Sometimes, you will learn,
Fools rush in.

Scene Twenty-Five

There's Juliet

Hip hop beatbox. Fun.

Paris *and the* **Capulets** *realise* **Juliet** *is alive – the wedding is
back on.*

Paris

She's alive
There's Juliet
They said that she had died
There's Juliet
She seems pretty fine
There's Juliet
That girl is mine!

Hello, Mister Capulet?
I've got some great news
I'll get straight to it
I just seen Juliet
At the window

I think she smiled at me bro
. . . I mean Dad
If I can call you that
We can get married today,
What do you say?
I can't believe

She's alive
There's Juliet!
They said that she had died
There's Juliet!
She seems pretty fine
There's Juliet!
That girl is mine!

Hello is that the Guardian?
I gotta great post you can put right in
In bold,
'Paris and Juliet to be married
With a horse and carriage'
You can put it on a website now?
You're so clever I wouldn't even know how
She's so lucky to get a top G like me
That's your quote
Her future's filled with hope!
Can't believe she's alive

She's alive
There's Juliet!
They said that she had died
There's Juliet!
She seems pretty fine
There's Juliet!
That girl is mine!
There's Juliet

Benvolio
It's been reported posted
That Paris and Juliet's wedding is on big

According to the Capulet's briefing
This wedding will go on this evening.

Scene Twenty-Six

Have a Say in This

Slow hip hop beatbox.

Juliet *tries to get hold of* **Romeo**, *she sees the wedding post and heads for the Northern Line.*

Juliet
Nah in print
I didn't think . . .
I never signed up for this
Never had a say in this
Never thought it would come to this
Everybody's gonna see this

Paris was the guy that I thought was harmless charmless,
ultimately witless
he's not the mastermind
Of any kind
Nah this is my dad
This is his plan

Ever since I was little
Raising me as stock
Ah now I should be grateful
That he's loosening the lock
In my name
He's in it for the power and the game
Did he ever love me or just pressured me for fame

I'm married to my Romeo
Yeh I want everyone to know
But gotta keep him alive
So I'm heading up the Northern Line
I beg he doesn't see the headlines

But when I try to text, all I get is one tick
Wanna hear his voice, hold his hand, I feel sick.

I'm gonna have a say in this
I'm taking control of this

Scene Twenty-Seven

Tube

Grime beatbox.

Romeo *has nothing to lose – he dies at the hands of Capulets.*
Juliet *risks her life.*

Romeo
Sitting on the Northern Line no reception
Can't believe all these thoughts in my mind
Was this deception?
Too much reflection
They're taking the mick
I gotta change at Kennington
As I reach my destination
Contemplate these neeks I'm facing
Capulets!
A whole bunch of Capulets!
I just wanna see Juliet
Twenty man whole gang of Capulets
Slowly lift my arm into the sky
Catch a few of their eyes
Their faces clearly surprised
They squeeze their triggers
With passion and vigour
So many bullets rain down
They can't miss
As I die
I picture me and Juliet in a kiss
Make death come quick
These damned rocks with speed they fly

Ready to die
O Capulet marksmen I am blessed
Shake the yoke of inauspicious stars
From this world wearied flesh

My Juliet is that really you

Juliet

My Romeo is this really you /

When you're number one.
When you're number one.

Shoot me then!
As you have shot him!
Feel my blood start to freeze
But nothing shall control me no more
I'm not a Capulet
I'm Juliet
Forever Romeo's
Where he go I go.

Benvolio

I'm sorry to announce that
The Northern Line won't run on time
Cos there was an intruder on the track
And it's a fact that
That passionate girl
Juliet Capulet
Has left this world.

Scene Twenty-Eight

Community

Freddy *reflects on what his community of Merton has become.*

All

Freddy we're at your door
Knock knock at the door

Freddy Freddy Freddy Freddy Freddy
Freddy we're –

Freddy

Don't knock anymore
That's not what my Community Centre's for

You sit in the middle of a place that calls itself a
community
But people come to escape 'cause outside's not what it
used to be
And usually I don't care
Let yourself in, pull up a chair
I have it easy compared to all those younger people out
there
When you're old you get really used to things and then
you get really scared
Because the younger folks won't do the things that you've
been doing for years
So you whisper in their ears – team Montague, over there
We don't like them, they hate us – if you're a Capulet –
over here
But love – love can be very loud.
It drowns everything out
If you switch off, you might even hear it

Juliet

I'll manage
/ If you help me to hide
Write a post online – 'Juliet has died'

Juliet *and* **Romeo**

Maybe I'm out of my mind

Juliet

/ If you help me to hide
I can be by Romeo's side

All

Have a good time
Sip a little wine

Coke and lime
And just chill out.

Scene Twenty-Nine

Epilogue – Star-Crossed Lovers

Record scratch, full underscore.

Actor 1

Two postcodes, two streets apart
In dear Merton where our story starts.

Actor 2

Beef from the past creates new tension.
Innocent blood spilled, they need an intervention.

Actor 3

A boy and a girl, supposed to be ops;
They chat, hold hands, secret meetings by the shops.

Actor 4

But these link ups are lamented, their lives are suspended:
Fam devastated but at least their war is ended.
(*Legato.*)

Actor 1

These two young youts who were really in love,
Their parents fighting, feuding fuming, all of the above,

Actor 2

Nothing could have stopped it, but the giving of their
hearts.
Welcome to this story and all of its parts.

Actor 3

If you wanna know the T then just lend us your ears;
We'll sing and rap and rhyme, it'll all become clear.

(*Sung.*)

Found one another,
Star-crossed lovers,
It wasn't to be.

Can't be together,
Love undercover,
Love is all they need.

A rose by any other name.

Found one another,
Star-crossed lovers,
It wasn't to be.